HEALING
IS
GOD'S WILL
FOR
EVERYONE!!

By Dwayne Norman

Empyrion Publishing
Winter Garden FL
EmpyrionPublishing.com

Healing is God's Will for Everyone
ISBN: 978-0692024577
Copyright 2014 by Dwayne Norman

Empyrion Publishing
Winter Garden FL
info@EmpyrionPublishing.com

Unless otherwise indicated, all Scripture quotations are taken from the New King James Version of the Bible.

Chapter 1

How to Determine God's Will for Healing

Some people's method for determining if God wants to heal them is to watch others who are sick. If they pray and get healed then the people assume it must be God's will, but if they don't get healed then it wasn't His will. A kind of hit and miss approach.

Some simple believe if God wants me healed then I'll be healed. If it happens it happens. That's what they mean when they say God is sovereign.

Some say that healing and miracles were only for the Bible days, and God doesn't do that anymore.

Many believe He can heal, but they're not sure if He wants to heal them. They don't know how to convince God to heal them.

Some think their disease is from the Lord, to teach them something, but they never learn what this mysterious lesson is.

Some don't believe the Lord will heal them because of their sinful life style. They don't understand the love and mercy of God.

Others think only "special" people get healed, and they don't know how to become one.

The favorite saying of some is, "You never know what God's going to do." Therefore, they have no faith that He will do anything for them.

Some think their sickness is a thorn sent to them they must bear, because they're so super spiritual.

Still others live daily with pain in their bodies, thinking it's a "blessing" from the Lord; not knowing it's a curse from the devil. Is it any wonder God said, **"My people are <u>destroyed</u> for lack of knowledge...?"** (Hosea 4:6). If sickness, disease and infection are not removed out of a person's body, it will destroy him. It never blesses, strengthens or makes better; only debilitates and consumes. The Lord lets us know that He doesn't want His people to be destroyed, but the way to prevent it, is to have the right kind of knowledge, then act upon it. So, it sounds to me that being destroyed or not being destroyed, is not a hit and miss thing. It also sounds like this is something that's left up to me; since it's based on my knowledge or lack thereof. I have a say so in whether I get destroyed or not. I therefore have a say so in whether I get healed or not. Would you agree? If you don't, just keep reading.

Mark 1:40-42 says,

"Now a leper came to Him, imploring Him, kneeling down to Him and saying to Him, "If You are willing, You can make me clean."

Then Jesus, moved with compassion, stretched out His hand and touched him, and said to him, "I am willing; be cleansed."

As soon as He had spoken, immediately the leprosy left him, and he was cleansed."

The leper said if you're willing, you can. It sounds like he knew Jesus had the ability or power to heal him, but he wasn't sure if He wanted to. That can prevent a person from being healed every time. It may seem like a minor point, but it's a very major (mountainous) problem in the Church today! You and I have to be totally convinced that God wants us healed. You cannot waver on this. You can't let your church friends, pastor or family members talk you out of it.

In the beginning of 2013, I had a similar experience with a person as Jesus did with the leper in Mark, chapter 1. I was invited to minister in 3 services at a church. I was told that one of the ladies (a believer) in the church had been diagnosed with cancer. The pastor said that everyone was believing God for her healing. The church was what I would call a Word of faith church. They believed in healing and miracles. I was told the doctors took a biopsy from under her arm and said they were 99% sure she had cancer. That's what the doctors told her and her husband. They were 99% sure. After the Sunday morning service, I ended up in a conversation with her while I was waiting on the Pastor to finish what he was doing. This lady told me she had only been "really" studying the Word for about 6 months; so she was pretty new to healing and walking by faith.

It seemed like she and everyone else had a good confession for her healing. Everybody was calling her healed in Jesus' Name. But after talking with her for about 10 minutes, she totally surprised me in a comment she made. She said, "I'm not really sure if it's God's will for me to be healed." When she said that I was reminded of the leper telling Jesus I know you can heal me if you're willing. When I heard that, my first thought was, "She's not even in faith for her healing, but everyone in the church probably thinks she is." I believe it was F.F. Bosworth, many years ago who said that faith can only be released where the will of God is known. Faith activates God's power to work in our lives. Jesus told many people they were healed, <u>according to their faith</u>.

If we're not convinced it's God's will for us to be healed, then we won't have any faith or confidence for our healing. So, I shared with her a number of different Scriptures about healing being God's will for her. If you want to know God's will, you must learn His Word. They're one and the same! I believe after our short conversation, she was convinced that God did want her healed. She and her husband were going back to the doctor the next day for another test. The doctors re-examined her and said they were 100% sure there was no cancer in her body! Praise the Lord! They went from 99% sure there was cancer to 100% sure there was none! God is so good to us! He wants all His children to be healed and walk in perfect health! That's His perfect will for us! Let's expect to experience it!

I believe one of the major reasons many Christians have not been healed today, is from a lack of confidence in God's will for them. We must be 100% convinced that healing is God's will for us! This is something we cannot waver on! I believe there are many Christians who say, "I believe God wants me healed", but aren't fully persuaded. They're just going through the motions, saying what they think they're supposed to say as people of faith. In their hearts they're still not sure. For our faith in healing to be strong and unwavering, we must meditate and study God's Word on healing until we have no doubts. Enough of the Word will drive all doubt out of our hearts, until all that's left is faith. Then no devil or person will be able to talk us out of our healing! But that takes time, and many Christians, it's sad to say, don't want to spend that much time in God's Word. If you're one of those types, and your healing doesn't come to pass, please don't blame the Lord. He had nothing to do with it! He wants you healed more than you do!

If I told my son I would buy him a car next month, he would probably get excited. Now, I'm taking into account that he trusts me and believes my word. What I told him I would do is a revelation of my will for him, that's why he would have faith or confidence that it would come to pass. I would create an excitement within him to tell other people. He would start telling his friends, "Next month I'm getting a new car." Now if he didn't know what my will was, he would not be expecting anything, but the more convinced he is that my word is true, the more excited he will be.

When the leper came to Jesus, he said I know you can (or you have the ability to) heal me, but I don't know if you want to. If my son knows I have the ability to buy him a car, but doesn't know I'm willing to, he still won't have faith for a car. Knowing that God can heal me is not enough. I must know that I know He's willing to heal me for faith to come.

Remember, faith comes by hearing God's Word (Romans 10:17). Hearing His Word is hearing what His will is for you. Also, knowing God's will doesn't make it automatically happen. Even though my son knows I will buy him a car next month, he still must believe and expect it to come to pass. Once you are convinced God's will is for you to be healed, you must release your faith, believe you receive it (whether you feel it or not) and start praising God, expecting it to come to pass!

Here is one of the main reasons you have to be thoroughly convinced that healing is God's will for you. This is why so many Christians have not received their healing, and I'm talking about Believers who said they knew it was His will for them. The devil knows that he has a greater chance of you doubting what God's will is for you, the longer it takes for your healing to come to pass. He knows if he can keep the pressure of pain and disease pounding in your body, day after day, then you might begin to wonder (just a little bit) if God really wants you healed. We all know what that's like. That's why we must stay in the Word. Keep feeding on faith and healing. While the devil tries to get you to doubt, you just keep getting stronger and stronger and stronger in your faith for healing. Like Abraham, you have to be and stay fully persuaded that what God has promised you, He is well able to perform it!

Romans 4:20,21 says:

"He did not waver at the promise of God through unbelief, but was strengthened in faith, giving glory to God, and being fully convinced that what He had promised He was also able to perform."

The devil's strategy is to do everything he can to get us to waver. Knowing that, we should do everything we can not to waver! I believe Abraham's faith got stronger and stronger because of two things. While the devil applied pressure to get him to doubt, he continued to give glory to God (before his miracle was manifested), and he was fully convinced or persuaded that what God had promised He was able to bring it to pass. To stay fully convinced meant that he had to keep confessing and going over God's promises to him; because faith comes by hearing the Word (Romans 10:17). If the devil never let off on the pressure, then Abraham couldn't let off on his faith pressure. Your faith in God applies pressure against what Satan is bringing against you. He likes to put pressure on us, let's put it back on him! Keep it applied until he caves in! He doesn't have anything strong enough to stop our faith from working! Every time we confess we're healed by Jesus' stripes, and every time we give God the glory, we're putting pressure on our enemy to loose his hold. If your healing doesn't come to pass instantly, keep applying the spiritual pressure. (See our book, "How to Respond to a Bad Report" for more teaching on releasing your faith).

Don't ever assume just because you haven't experienced God's will (healing) for your body that it's not His will. Our experiences are not the determining factors of what God's will is; only His Word determines that. His Word reveals to us that Salvation is His perfect will for all people (John 3:16; I Timothy 2:4; II Peter 3:9). Even though He doesn't want anyone to go to Hell, many people will still go. Those that go to Hell do not prove, by their experience, that salvation isn't His will for everyone. It just proves that many won't receive His will done in their lives. The same is true for healing, prosperity and receiving any blessings from the Lord. Once we know what His Will is for us, we must release faith and receive. Many times when Jesus ministered to people, He would tell them according to your faith be it unto you. He never said according to my faith (as Jesus). In other words, He was saying what will come to pass in your life, will be according to your faith; what you can believe for. Wow! That puts the pressure on me to develop my faith. I'm going to have to spend time in the Word. He never said according to your spouse's faith, the pastor's faith or the guest ministers faith be it unto you. They can add their faith to yours, but the main determining factor is your faith. The Lord Jesus had perfect faith, but He never said His faith was more than enough for them. He never said, "You don't need any faith. I have plenty."

Because God is no respecter of persons, I see Him (in my mind's eye) saying, "Dwayne, according to your faith be it unto you." Whether I like it or not, the blessings I experience from the Lord will be mainly based on what I can believe for. I don't have a right to put anything off on anyone else. I don't have a right to blame the devil (because he's defeated) or anyone else if I don't receive God's will in my life. Again, for every one of us, let's remember; according to our faith be it unto us.

There are many Scriptures on healing in the Bible. I'm not going to write them all in this book, but I want to remind you of three major ones.

Isaiah 53:4,5 says:

"Surely He has borne our griefs and carried our sorrows; yet we esteemed Him stricken, smitten by God, and afflicted.

But He was wounded for our transgressions, He was bruised for our iniquities; the chastisement for our peace was upon Him and by His stripes we are healed."

Jesus bore our griefs and sorrows, but in the

Hebrew language in which this was written, grief also means <u>sickness</u>, and sorrow means <u>pain</u>. We know from John 3:16 that Jesus died for the whole world, all people. Therefore, when it says He bore "our" sicknesses and pains; that is referring to everyone. When it says "we" are healed, that is referring to everyone included in the word "our"! Through Jesus' 39 stripes and His death on the cross, He bore and defeated everyone's sicknesses and pains. And in their place, He has obtained healing for everyone. In other words, if you're sick right now, you need to know that God has <u>already healed you</u>. Even if you're body says you're sick, God says you're healed; and if you'll start believing and agreeing with God (His Word), you can experience your healing! I didn't say and God didn't say, if you'll agree with Him one time, you'll instantly be healed, that's very possible, but it doesn't always happen that way. You and I have to keep confessing, in faith, what the Word says (not how we feel in our bodies) over our bodies until enough power is released out of that Word to change our bodies!

This isn't mind over matter. You're not denying that your body is sick and feels bad. What the doctor told you is true according to his examinations. That's the truth in the natural realm, and it's really true, but there is a higher truth than that. God's Word is spiritual truth, and what He says He's done for you in

Christ always trumps (overrides) what man and our flesh say! As Believers, we're all in the same boat, so to speak. We all must operate in faith to receive what was done for us at Calvary. Listen! You don't have to walk by faith if you don't want to, but the only other way to walk is by unbelief. Hebrews 11:6 tells us we <u>cannot</u> please God without faith. We must believe that He is, not just that He exists, but that He is a right now God, and that He will reward us when we diligently seek Him. We need to really believe that!

Matthew 8:16,17 says:

"When evening had come, they brought to Him many who were demon-possessed. And He cast out the spirits with a word, and healed all who were sick,

that it might be fulfilled which was spoken by Isaiah the prophet, saying: "He himself took our infirmities and bore our sicknesses.""

Let me tell you one thing I like about Matthew's account. It's a commentary from the Holy Spirit through Matthew of Isaiah 53:4. If you weren't sure that the Hebrew word for "grief" is sickness, the Holy Spirit led Matthew to translate it from the original Hebrew. This is one verse we don't need to look up a man's commentary on, because God gave us His own. Verse 16 tells us the reason Jesus could deliver the people and heal the sick. It was to fulfill Isaiah's prophecy. If we weren't healed by Jesus' stripes, if we weren't healed because He bore all of our sicknesses and diseases, then He couldn't have healed all who were sick. You don't have to be a rocket scientist to figure that one out.

I Peter 2:24 says:

Who Himself bore our sins in His own body on the tree, that we, having died to sins, might live for righteousness-by whose stripes you were healed."

This was written after Jesus took the 39 stripes for us, died and arose from the dead. The Apostle Paul said, **"...By the mouth of two or three witnesses every word shall be established."** (II Corinthians 13:1) The reason most Christians believe that salvation is God's will for everyone, is from being taught that way. They've heard Scriptures like: John 3:16,17; I Timothy 2:4; II Peter 3:9 that reveal to us that God doesn't want anyone to perish. They've heard these verses so much in their churches that their faith has developed very strong in the area of salvation (remember, faith comes by hearing the Word - Romans 10:17). But when it comes to healing, they've heard very little teaching from the Scriptures in this area, so their faith is very weak when it comes to Divine healing. They don't have a problem with me saying, "God doesn't want anyone to go to Hell," but they get very bothered if I say, "God doesn't want anyone to be sick."

The very same Bible that proves God's will is salvation for all people, proves healing is God's will for all people. You either believe all God said is true or you don't believe any of it! Your choice! If you're going to a church that doesn't believe this way, then know this, their doubt doesn't change the integrity of God's Word! You need to get in a church that believes the whole Bible, and not just the part they or their denomination wants to believe! If you would spend as much time meditating on healing Scriptures as you have about salvation your faith would soar like an eagle, and the devil would not be able to shake you when it comes to healing!

CHAPTER
2

THINGS JESUS NEVER
SAID TO THE SICK

I heard one minister teaching some things about God's will being revealed through Jesus in the four Gospels, and it blessed me greatly. I want to share it with you. First, I want to look at a couple of Scriptures.

Hebrews 1:3 says:

"Who (Jesus) being the brightness of His glory and <u>the express image</u> of His person, and upholding all things by the word of His power, when He had by Himself purged our sins, sat down at the right hand of the Majesty on high."

John 6:38 says:

"For I have come down from heaven, not to do My own will, but the will of Him who sent Me."

This is so important! Never forget this! When the Lord Jesus walked this earth He fully represented the Father God. He was the express image of God in the flesh, in a human body. He said He did not come to do His will, but the will of the Father. That means, everything He said and did in the four Gospels was the will of the Father. It was a manifestation of God's will to man. Therefore, if we will spend enough time studying all the healings, deliverances and miracles Jesus did in His ministry, then we'll know what God's will is for us in those areas. Think about this with me. Because Jesus only said and did God's perfect will all the time, then anything else you read in the Bible that doesn't seem to line up with that (in your mind), means you must have a lack of understanding somewhere. You can never take other Scriptures and prove that something Jesus said was incorrect. He **never** missed it!! He was the expressed will of God in the earth! If I'm reading about Job, the thorn Paul dealt with or something else, and don't understand it; then I need to go read again all that Jesus did for the people in His ministry.

Please study this out for yourself. Get your Bible and read every healing, deliverance and miracle the

Lord did in the four Gospels. Listen closely! Not one time did a sick person come to Jesus, and He said, "I'm not going to heal you because you're like Job." Christians will say that today about themselves, but Jesus never did; and He was the perfect will of God for all mankind. Not one time did a sick person come to Jesus, and He said, "I'm not going to heal you because you're sickness is a thorn that's been given to you." Christians will say that today about themselves, but Jesus never did; and He was the perfect will of God for all mankind. Usually, Christians will say things like that because they're tired of waiting for their healing to come to pass, they're starting to doubt if it's God's will; so they try to come up with other reasons why they're not healed. Reasons that will still make them look "spiritual", without sounding like they're wavering in their faith. The thorn that came to Paul was because of the many revelations he had, and the Bible says it was a messenger from Satan, and not from God. The devil tried to stop him from preaching the Gospel that God revealed to him. God did not give him the thorn, but He did give him all power over the devil; and Paul fulfilled God's will for his life.

Remember, it was the devil (the destroyer), who came to God wanting Him to hurt Job, but God wouldn't do it. He said to the devil, **"Behold, all that he has is in your power; only do not lay a hand on**

his person. So Satan went out from the presence of the Lord." (Job 1:12) What did the devil do when he went out from the presence of the Lord? He (the devil) went down to the earth and attacked Job. God didn't attack him, the devil did. Satan is the one who brings sickness and pain, and he's been attacking man ever since then. God is the one who heals!

Here's what you're probably thinking now, "Well if God didn't do it, then He allowed it." I hear this phrase used by Christians all the time. They'll say God "allowed it", to imply that He had something to do with it. Like saying the head of the Mafia allowed one of his men to murder someone. Even though he didn't do it, he's still just as guilty; since he had someone else to do it for him. According to the Bible, that's not what we mean when we say God allows something. If God allows something to happen in a person's life, it means He did not stop it from coming to pass. If God removes His hand of protection from a person, it doesn't mean He had anything to do with what happened to them. Let's not implicate the Lord in our lack of faith or ignorance. God will never get the devil to attack someone so He can keep His hands clean. As human beings, we have a free will. We can do whatever we want to, and you could say God will allow it. If you want to go to the Post Office, God will allow it; but that just means He won't stop you from going. To say God allowed you to go to the Post

Office doesn't mean He had anything to do with it. It just means He didn't intervene and stop you from going. Let me give you another example. In Deuteronomy 28:1- 14, God told Israel that all His blessings would come on them if they diligently obeyed His voice and followed His commandments. But in verse 15, He said if you don't obey My voice and follow My commandments, then all these curses will come on you.

The curses were already in the world around them. God didn't say He would send the curses on them. The Lord was simply telling them what they needed to do to give Him the right to protect them from the curses. God didn't say, "If you obey My voice and commandments, I still may allow the curses to come on you." No! He would have to break His promise for that to happen, and it's impossible for God to lie (Numbers 23:19; Titus 1:2; Hebrews 6:18)! God was telling them, "There's a lot of sickness, poverty and death out there, but you can live free from them by obeying My Word. But remember, if you don't obey My Word, then you (not God, and not God allowing it) will open up a door for those bad things to come on you. It will be your fault." If you say God allowed it, it doesn't mean He had anything to do with it. Through their disobedience, they stopped the Lord from protecting them from the curse. So, you could say God allowed the curse to come on them, but that doesn't mean He had anything to do with it. They held God's hand of blessing back through their unbelief. What God was allowing, was for them to exercise their free will to choose to disobey Him, thereby forcing Him to stand back and watch the curse come on them. Then, according to His Word, He did not have a legal right to intervene in their situation. They tied His hands through their disobedience, so He could not help them. They were stopping God from helping them through their lack of faith and trust, which gave the devil more freedom to attack them.

Then those very Christians will say, "I wonder why God allowed this to happen?" He didn't allow it! He had nothing to do with it! He could not intervene in your situation because you closed the door off to His help. Again, He had to allow it to happen, meaning He did not have the legal right to step in and stop it, without breaking His Word. If you choose to rob a bank, get caught and go to jail; don't say that God allowed you to go to jail. Yes, it's true that He didn't stop you from going to jail, but that's not because it was His will for you to go to jail. You did that to yourself. So, don't imply He had anything to do with it. Don't try to spiritualize it and make it sound like it fits into some higher Divine plan for your life; because it doesn't. Any of us can open a door to the devil through unbelief and disobedience. If we do, let's not turn around and blame God for it, because we don't want to admit we missed it. Don't insinuate that God had something to do with your problem, by saying He allowed it! God is not mocked!

"Do not be deceived, God is not mocked; for whatever a man sows, that he will also reap.

For he who sows to his flesh will of the flesh reap corruption, but he who sows to the Spirit will of the Spirit reap everlasting life." (Galatians 6:7,8)

The Lord said if you and I sow to the flesh we will of the flesh reap corruption. If we then declare that God allowed us to reap corruption; that would be a lie. Even though He didn't stop the corruption from coming, He still had nothing to do with us reaping it. Do you see that? If we had not sown to the flesh, the corruption would not have come.

Here's another area we need to have better clarity on. The devil comes against Christians for 2 main reasons: 1: Because they are serving the Lord. 2: Because they are not serving the Lord. If you notice, the attacks will come no matter which category you're in, so don't be surprised. Don't ever assume that the attacks from the devil only come to Christians who have sinned. If you are serving God with all your heart, I guarantee that the devil will try to stop you. But remember what Paul said in Ephesians, Chapter 6, we can quench all the fiery darts of the devil with our shield of faith!

A third area, in which all of us have opened up a door for problems in our lives, is from our own making. It's called not using wisdom or common sense. We have committed this mistake many times, but thank God for His mercy. Think about this with me. Picture a Christian driving down the highway talking on his cell phone. He accidentally drops it in the floor of the car, then (while still driving) starts looking around the floor for it. Without realizing it, he drives right off the road into a tree and is killed. Here is what most of the Church would say, "The devil killed him or God took him. Or, I wonder why God allowed him to die?" None of those statements would be correct. He died because he wasn't paying attention to his driving. There was no spiritual significance for his death, but Christians would be forever speculating on why he died; trying to find a higher meaning. Some would say his death might have been the result of sin in his life or a lack of faith. It was neither one. The only reason he died was because of a dumb mistake, but no one will ever know that, because he took that truth to the grave with him. No matter how strongly we walk and live by faith, we still must walk in wisdom and use good common sense.

Not one time did Jesus tell a sick person that He wasn't going to heal him because God was allowing him to be sick for a special reason. <u>Not one time</u> in Matthew, Mark, Luke or John did anyone come to Jesus for healing, and He said "It wasn't God's will to heal him." When the Lord told the leper it was His will to heal him, that's never changed. If He's willing to save one person, He's willing to save them all (if they'll receive it). If He's willing to heal one person, He's willing to heal them all (if they'll receive it). Jesus shows no partiality! He's the same yesterday, today and forever (Hebrews 13:8)!

Forever, the Lord Jesus has revealed to us God's will concerning healing. He's our standard to go by in life. You could say He's our measuring rod. We are to judge everything by Him. All of God's Word, if you understand it correctly, will agree with what He said and did. Now listen, Job was not our standard. The Apostle Paul was not our standard. Yes, they were great men of God. Paul even said to follow him as he followed Christ (The Standard for life). So, if I'm studying something in the Bible that seems to contradict what Jesus said in the Gospels, then I need to stop and make this judgment call. I need to say to myself, "I know that Jesus revealed God's perfect will for all mankind, and what I'm studying doesn't seem (to me) to agree with that; therefore, I must be missing it somewhere. I <u>never</u> assume I'm right and Jesus was wrong. I always acknowledge there must be something I don't understand in this story. I begin to pray and ask the Lord to reveal to me what I'm missing, because the correct understanding will always agree with God's revealed will through Jesus in the 4 Gospels.

That's why in my studying and meditating, I spend a lot of time looking at all the healings, deliverances and miracles of Jesus. I also spend time reading all of the letters (epistles) written to the Church. These letters should be just as real to us as the mail we get out of our mail box every day. The big difference is, these letters are written to us from God.

One pastor told me that a couple came to him to discuss joining his church, but before they would, he had to pass their test. They were going to ask him a question, and the answer he gave them would determine if they would become part of his church. The question was about a very close relative who died of a disease. They told the pastor how this lady was a wonderful Christian and loved God with all her heart. They spoke about how strong in faith she was. They assumed, since she was one of the pillars of the church, and still died, that it must have been God's will. They wanted to know what the pastor thought. He let them know that he couldn't lie to them, even if they didn't come to his church. He told them he didn't know why she died, but that it wasn't God's will. He wanted her healed. After hearing his answer, they never came to his church again.

Not one time did Jesus ever tell a sick person that God was going to heal him, because he loved the Lord with all his heart, is a wonderful man of God and is constantly helping people everywhere he goes. Do you know why? Because as much as we don't like to admit it, healing doesn't ever come because of our good works. Good works are great and important. The Bible says people will know we are Christians by our love for them. As true as that is, it does not earn us healing. Here is one of the main excuses I here from Christians who doubt that God wants to heal everyone. They'll say, "Sister Sally died of cancer, and she was a saint. She baked cakes, pies, fed the poor, gave all of her money to the church and supported an unwed mother's home. There was no one more spiritual and Godly than Sally. If anyone was going to get healed, it would have been her." Please pay close attention here. If you examine what they said about sister Sally, everything was based on works (yes, good works, but still works). They were implying that God owed her healing, but He didn't!

It's so easy, if you're serving the Lord with all your heart, going to church every time the doors open, reading your Bible every day, constantly praying and walking in love, to feel that God should definitely heal you. The devil wants you think, "I know I'll get healed, because the Lord knows how faithful I've been to him." We must never allow ourselves to think this way, because that's just a deceptive form of pride. Yes, God will reward faithfulness, but not because we're earning something from Him. We can't earn healing, just like we can't earn salvation. They only come by faith, so that it can be freely from His grace. I hear this everywhere I go, "Brother so and so died of a terrible disease, and he was a good man. I guess it was God's will. If anyone deserved to be healed, it was him." Listen! No one deserves to be saved or healed. All of our goodness and righteousness apart from Jesus is as filthy rags. No matter how good and holy I act, I can't earn my healing. Like Jesus said to people, according to your faith be it unto you. God will bless us for all our good works, but the only way to receive from Him is by faith. We can't please Him without it!

Many times Jesus would tell people that their faith has made them whole, and be it unto you as you have believed. He never said according to My (Jesus) faith be healed. He never said I have perfect faith, we'll just use mine. He never said according to your good works be healed. He never said according to how much you feed the poor be healed. He never said according to your faithfulness to attend church be healed. He never said according to how much you help in your community be healed. He never said according to how much you love God be healed. All those things are very good, but Jesus never said that all things are possible to him who loves God and does good works. He said, **"All things are possible to him who believes."** (Mark 9:23) God has really brought me back to the fact that if I'm not enjoying the blessings of Heaven, it's not anyone's fault but mine. As human beings, we like to blame other people if something isn't working right for us. But when it comes to receiving from the Lord, the only one to blame, if things aren't working the way I want them to, is myself. That's why I spend lots of time meditating and hearing the Word (Romans 10:17). If I want to have strong muscles, I need to spend a lot of time exercising. If I want to have strong faith, I need to spend a lot of time spiritually exercising. When other Christians don't want to take the time to do that, I'm not daunted. I've made up my mind, I'm going to be strong in faith, whether anyone else is or not. If all of us had that kind of attitude, we would be running the devil off all of the time!

A number of years ago, a good friend of mine died of cancer. This lady was definitely one of the pillars in her church. She seemed to be one of the most spiritually mature women of God that I knew. After she died, a friend of mine who was very close to her made this comment; "Even though she died, I know she had faith for healing." I got to thinking about what he said, and it didn't make any sense, according to

God's Word. Think about how this sounds to you. What if I said, "I know a lady that went to Hell, but she definitely had faith for salvation"? You would probably say, "If she really had faith for salvation, she would be saved." That's right! The way to receive healing is to operate in faith. If she truly was operating in faith for her healing it would come to pass. Now, if you're starting to wonder about what I just said; let's go back to our standard or measuring rod. Let's go back to the One who revealed to us God's perfect will concerning healing. Not one time did Jesus ever tell a sick person, "You're still going to die even though you have faith for healing." Let me use me, as an example, so I don't make anyone mad. If I think I have strong faith for healing, but my healing has not come to pass, then I need to examine my faith. I need to continue to build my faith up, because it may not be as strong as I thought it was, or there may be another area I'm lacking understanding in. One example is: the Bible says that faith works by love (Galatians 5;6). If I think my faith is working great, but I'm not walking in love, then I've been deceived.

Not one time did Jesus ever tell a sick person, "I don't know if you're going to be healed or not, because God is sovereign. You never know what He's going to do." The Lord never told anyone that, so why do Christians tell people that today, when it comes to healing. Again, they don't say it when it comes to salvation, because they know from the Word, God doesn't want anyone to parish. If they studied the Word enough about healing, they would know that God doesn't want anyone to be sick. Also, most Christians don't understand what it means to say that God is sovereign. The word "sovereign" in the dictionary means having supreme rank or power, self-governing. Yes, God does have supreme rank and power. He's the true and one and only God. When many say God is sovereign concerning healing, they're implying that sometimes the Lord may want you healed and sometimes He may want you sick, you just never know. Again, those who believe that way haven't read God's Word (His will). They don't know that God has revealed to us in the Scriptures exactly what His will is when it comes to healing. His mind has been made up! He doesn't waver back and forth! The Christians who say that are usually the ones who are getting about half mad at God because their healing isn't manifested yet, and they're trying to find a reason for the delay without blaming themselves. They don't want to dare say it may be because of <u>their</u> lack of faith. They will exhaust every possible reason before they come to that conclusion. Ultimately, what it comes down to for you and me, is according to <u>your</u> faith be it unto you. We can't get away from that, so let's quit trying.

It's true that God is sovereign. He's omnipotent. Everything is possible for Him, but He <u>can't</u> and <u>will not</u> do anything contrary to His Word. He and His Word are one (John 1:1,14). Everything He does is always in the boundaries of His revealed will in His Word. Here are 3 things God can't do: 1. He can't change (Hebrews 13:8). 2. He can't tempt anyone with evil (James 1:13). 3. He can't lie (Numbers 23:19; Titus 1:2; Hebrews 6:18). So, when I say God is sovereign, I'm saying He will always use His omnipotence and all His resources to back any child of God who believes and obeys His Word! When you make up your mind that you're going to stand firm on His Word for healing, there's not a thing the devil can do to stop it from coming to pass! The sovereign, Almighty God is on your side! One of His Names is Jehovah Rapha, the Lord who heals you! Expect your healing to come to pass in Jesus' Name!!

Think about this. <u>Not one time</u> did Jesus ever tell a sick person, "God is not going to heal you because of sin in your life." Many Christians have struggled to receive their healing because they feel they don't measure up. That's another way of saying they don't deserve it. They don't feel close to the Lord, so they think they're not worthy to be healed. Listen! If healing was based on <u>our</u> worthiness, no one would be healed. We've already talked about this some, but I want to go a little further with it. We are only worthy through the Blood of Jesus. It's not by our stripes that we're healed. It's by <u>His</u> stripes. Step up and receive all that Jesus did for you, and don't let the devil steal it from you! Look at this story in John 9:1-7.

"Now as Jesus passed by, He saw a man who was blind from birth.

And His disciples asked Him, saying, "Rabbi, who sinned, this man or his parents, that he was born blind?"

Jesus answered, "Neither this man nor his parents sinned, but that the works of God should be revealed in him.

I must work the works of Him who sent Me while it is day; the night is coming when no one can work.

As long as I am in the world, I am the light of the world."

When He had said these things, He spat on the ground and made clay with the saliva; and He anointed the eyes of the blind man with the clay.

And He said to him, "Go, wash in the pool of Siloam" (which is translated, Sent). So he went and washed, and came back seeing."

First, let me say this. Don't assume that every time a Christian is sick, he must have committed a sin. This is exactly what Jesus' disciples assumed. You can tell by what they said, that they were not open to any other answer, but what they thought. They thought they were so smart, yet they got it totally wrong. They assumed (we need to watch assuming too much-always thinking we're right) there could be only 2 reasons he was blind from birth. Either he sinned, and it would have to have been in his mother's womb, since he was blind from birth; or his parents sinned. Jesus shot down both of those theories, but he didn't tell them why the man was blind. He did say that the works of God should be revealed in him. The works of God were not blindness; because He went on to do those works by healing him. If blindness was the work of God, He would not have healed him, because He would have come against His Father's perfect will. But He did the Father's perfect will by healing him.

Even when Jesus ministered healing to people, in whom sin was the cause of their sickness, He didn't tell them their sin would stop them from being healed.

John 5:2-9,14 says:

"Now there is in Jerusalem by the Sheep Gate a pool, which is called in Hebrew, Bethesda, having five porches.

In these lay a great multitude of sick people, blind, lame, paralyzed, waiting for the moving of the water.

For an angel went down at a certain time into the pool and stirred up the water; then whoever stepped in first, after the stirring of the water, was made well of whatever disease he had.

Now a certain man was there who had an infirmity thirty-eight years.

When Jesus saw him lying there, and knew that he already had been in that condition a long time, He said to him, "Do you want to be made well?"

The sick man answered Him, "Sir, I have no man to put me into the pool when the water is stirred up; but while I am coming, another steps down before me."

Jesus said to him, "Rise, take up your bed and walk."

And immediately the man was made well, took up his bed, and walked. And that day was the Sabbath.

Afterward Jesus found him in the temple, and said to him, "See, you have been made well. <u>Sin no more</u>, lest a worse thing come upon you.""

This man had this disease (infirmity) for 38 years. It sounds to me that Jesus revealed to him why he had been sick all those years. He said it was because of sin in his life. If there was no sin in his life, Jesus would not have told him to go sin no more. He went so far as to say, if you go back to whatever this sin was and continue in it, you'll end up physically worse than you've been for these last 38 years. My point though, was that Jesus did not say anything about his sin, before He healed him. Isn't that interesting? Many ministers today would not have ministered healing to the man without first convincing him to repent, renounce his sin, and probably spend a little time counseling with him first. Why didn't Jesus do it that way? Because when God heals someone, He also forgives him or her at the same time. When He forgives someone, He also heals him at the same time. Let's read Matthew 9:2-7.

"Then behold, they brought to Him a paralytic lying on a bed. When Jesus saw their faith, He said to the paralytic, "Son, be of good cheer; your sins are forgiven you."

And at once some of the scribes said within themselves, "This Man blasphemes!"

But Jesus, knowing their thoughts, said, "Why do you think evil in your hearts?

For which is easier, to say, 'Your sins are forgiven you,' or to say, 'Arise and walk'?

But that you may know that the Son of Man has power on earth to forgive sins-then He said to the paralytic, "Arise, take up your bed, and go to your house."

And he arose and departed to his house."

This was a case where Jesus knew (by the Spirit of God) this man was being condemned by the devil for some kind of sin, which could have hindered him from releasing faith for his healing. I John 3:21 says, **"Beloved, if our heart does not condemn us, we have confidence toward God."** Therefore, the opposite is true. If your heart is condemning you, then it will be difficult to have confidence or faith toward God. The scribes didn't believe the man's sins had been forgiven. It's not something you can see with your natural eyes. So, Jesus demonstrated that he was forgiven by using the same power to heal the man. I believe when the Lord forgave this man, He also healed Him. The man didn't realize it, so Jesus demonstrated it for him. It seems that forgiveness and healing are tied together. This is a revelation we've had very little teaching on, but Jesus understood it. The Apostle James understood it also. James 5:14,15 says:

"Is anyone among you sick? Let him call for the elders of the church, and let them pray over him, anointing him with oil in the name of the Lord.

And the prayer of faith will save the sick, and the Lord will raise him up. And if he has committed sins, he will be forgiven."

Notice, the prayer of faith will save or heal the sick person, and then he throws this in: if he has committed sins, he will be forgiven. It didn't say anything about him confessing his sins, or telling anyone that he committed any sins. It's like saying something in passing. And by the way, when the Lord heals him, He will also forgive him if he's committed any sins. He may have thought that healing was all he could receive through the prayer of faith, but he got cleansed as well. Look again at Matthew 9:5, **"For which is easier, to say, 'Your sins are forgiven you,' or to say, 'arise and walk'?"** The Lord wasn't just saying it's as easy to forgive as it is to heal, but He was implying that He always does both. We know the man was a paralytic. He needed to be healed, but it's as if Jesus was saying, "It doesn't matter which one of these declarations of faith I make to him, both will come to pass in his life. If He says you're healed, then you're forgiven also. If He says you're forgiven, then you're healed also. I just wanted to give you something that I believe warrants further meditation. It seems there's more here than we've understood. We need to spend more time studying the healing and miracle ministry of Jesus. I want to look at something else brought out in Luke's account of the healing of the paralytic.

"Now it happened on a certain day, as He was

teaching, that there were Pharisees and teachers of the law sitting by, who had come out of every town of Galilee, Judea, and Jerusalem. And <u>the power of the Lord was present to heal them.</u>"

It sounds like Jesus had a big crowd at this particular meeting. He had religious leaders and teachers of the law (lawyers?) from 3 different areas. We know that the place was so packed they had to let the paralytic down through the roof to get to Jesus. It must have been wall to wall people, but we only have record of 1 man being healing. Yet, the Bible says the power of the Lord was present to heal <u>them.</u> God's healing power was there to heal all of them, not just the paralytic man, but no one else was healed. Why? Even if the power is present to heal, faith is still required. It sounds like we're back to: according to <u>your faith</u> be it unto you. According to the Scriptures, the paralytic man was the only one who operated in faith to receive. Even though it was God's will to heal all these people, they were not automatically healed. <u>Not one time</u> did Jesus ever say to a sick person, "You will automatically be healed today, because God's will is healing for you."

After ministering in a church in St. Louis in 2012, I received a wonderful testimony from a lady who was in the Sunday morning service. I had taught on the power in the message of the cross (see our book, The

Awesome Power in the Message of the Cross). I asked everyone that was sick or in pain to stand up. I explained that the power of the Lord was present to heal them, but they needed to release their faith and expect to receive. This lady told me later that she had been having pain in her side and breast area. She said that one of her relatives or close friends had died of breast cancer, and that the devil had been attacking her with thoughts in her mind that she would die also. She said as soon as she stood up and expected to receive, all of the pain left immediately. Now, she had been to the doctors for test to be run a few days before that Sunday service. The day after this service, the doctor had the results from the test. He said that there were nodules in her breast. Well, she did not receive that because she knew she was healed in the service, so she went back to the doctor to have new tests run. When the results came in, the doctor said they could not find any nodules or evidence of cancer, Praise the Lord!

There are gifts of healings that can go into operation also, and people who seem to have no faith at all can be healed, but there's not always a set time and place when that will happen. You may die before experiencing that, so you need to develop your faith now. Sometimes, people who have been healed that way, end up losing their healing, because they don't know how to operate in faith. It takes faith in God to keep your healing and to walk in perfect health, because the devil will try his best to steal it from you.

Acts 10:38

"How God anointed Jesus of Nazareth with the Holy Spirit and with power, who went about doing good and healing all who were oppressed by the devil, for God was with Him."

This verse tells me that every where Jesus went He did good, therefore God's will is always good for people. It also tells me that all sickness and disease is Satanic oppression, not Godly oppression. God doesn't oppress people, but the devil does. If you are sick right now, the one attacking you is the devil, and you have power in Jesus' Name to command him to leave (James 4:7). It's not God's will for you to be sick, if you think it is, then why would you take medicine and go to the doctor to get well? If you really think your disease is God's will and you want to do His will, then according to that reasoning, you should do your best to stay sick. Any effort to get well would be coming against what you believe is God's will for your life. Can you see how ridiculous that sounds? No Believers would ever think that way if they spent enough time in God's Word getting their minds renewed to the perfect will of the Lord concerning healing. The more time we spend in the

Word, the more that Word will cleanse our minds of all squirrelly and unbelief thinking! God's will is healing and prosperity for everyone, and He will do everything He can to bring that to pass, when His children cooperate with Him in faith. Let me leave you with one last point, something I want to reiterate.

<u>Not one time</u> did Jesus ever tell a sick person, "I'm going to heal you, even though you have no faith for healing; because you've prayed, fasted, done so many good things for people and you really love God." Again, this may be the number one reason why so many Christians feel that God should heal them. It's always based on good works. In the Church, we're taught to produce good works for the Lord, and rightly so. But we're not reminded enough that our good works don't merit anything from the Lord. We serve the Lord with all of our hearts because He's worthy of it, and He blesses us because we're obeying His Word, but never earning anything. Everything we receive from Him is freely from His grace through faith. Do you remember the story of the Centurion's servant who was sick? He sent his elders to go plead with Jesus for healing for his servant.

"And when they came to Jesus, they begged Him earnestly, saying that the one for whom He should do this was deserving, for he loves our nation, and has built us a synagogue.

Then Jesus went with them. And when He was already not far from the house, the centurion sent friends to Him, saying to Him, "Lord, do not trouble Yourself, for I am not worthy that You should enter under my roof.

Therefore I did not even think myself worthy to come to You. But say the word, and my servant will be healed." (Luke 7:4-7)

The elders are the ones who said the Centurion was worthy. They started bragging about his good works. I don't believe the Centurion told them to say that, because of verse 6. Before Jesus arrived at his house, he sent friends to Him, and revealed his true motives. He told the Lord that he wasn't even worthy for Him to come under his roof. That doesn't sound like a man that thinks he deserves something from the Lord. I believe Jesus went with them, because He was so eager to heal people, and the man asked for healing for his servant. It wasn't because of his good works. The Centurion was operating in great faith! He told the Lord that he just believed His Word, and that would be enough! We need to follow his example! Let's get enough Word in us, where we can say, "Lord, I believe your Word, and I expect it to come to pass in my life!" His Word will never fail us! It works in us mightily! Healing is the children's bread, and we're the children, and the devil can't have our bread! <u>Always stay in the Word,</u> <u>that's where the</u> <u>victory is at</u>!!

About the Author

Dwayne Norman is a 1978 graduate of Christ For The Nations Bible Institute in Dallas, Texas. He spent 3 years witnessing to prostitutes and pimps in the red light district of Dallas, and another 3 years ministering as a team leader in the Campus Challenge ministry of Dr. Norvel Hayes. He was ordained by Pastor Buddy and Pat Harrison of Faith Christian Fellowship in Tulsa, Oklahoma in September 1980, and is part of Dr. Ed Dufresne's Fresh Oil Fellowship. He also taught evangelism classes several times at Dr. Hayes' Bible school in Tennessee.

Soon the Lord led him to go on the road ministering. He ministers powerfully on soul winning, and on how God wants to use all Believers in demonstrating His Kingdom not just in Word but also in Power!

He teaches with clarity, the work that God accomplished for all believers in Christ from the cross to the throne, and the importance of this revelation to the church for the fulfillment of Jesus' commission to make disciples of all nations.

He strongly believes that we are called to do the works Jesus did and greater works in His Name, not just in church but especially in the market place. As a result Dwayne experiences many healing miracles in his services, arms and legs growing out, as well as other miracles.

He and his wife Leia travel and teach Supernatural Evangelism and train Believers in who they are in Christ and how to operate in their ministries.

To inquire for meetings with Dwayne & Leia Norman, please contact them at:

Dwayne & Leia Norman
124 Evergreen Court
Mt. Sterling, KY 40353

(859) 351-6496
dwayne7@att.net
Web: www.dwaynenormanministries.org

Contact Dwayne to order his other books and products:

The Mystery DVD's (12 hours)	$50.00
The Mystery (book)	$15.00
The Mystery Study Guide	$10.00
The Awesome Power in the Message of the Cross	$10.00
Your Beginning with God	$10.00
The Law of the Spirit of Life in Christ Jesus	$10.00
Demonstrating God's Kingdom	$10.00

www.ingramcontent.com/pod-product-compliance
Lightning Source LLC
Chambersburg PA
CBHW061200040426
42445CB00013B/1755